T0083702

The Rules of
ASSOCIATION FOOTBALL
1863

Foreword by Sir Bobby Charlton

Introduction by Melvyn Bragg

Bodleian Library
UNIVERSITY OF OXFORD

First published in 2006 by the Bodleian Library
Broad Street, Oxford, OX1 3BG

www. bodleianbookshop.co.uk

ISBN 1 85124 375 5
ISBN 13 978 1 85124 375 4

The Bodleian Library is grateful to The FA for their cooperation
and supply of materials towards the production of this book.

Design by Melanie Gradtke
Printed and bound by The University Press, Cambridge
A CIP record of this publication is available from the British
Library

Images on pp. 4, 8, 17, 22, 32 are from *The Graphic*, December
1872. Bodleian Library, N.2288 b.7.

Contents

DRIBBLING

Acknowledgements

This book owes its existence to the good will, cooperation and effort of many individuals. We are grateful to Sir Bobby Charlton for writing the Foreword. It was in Melvyn Bragg's *12 Books That Changed the World* published by Hodder & Stoughton © 2006 that the universal significance of the First Rule Book became apparent; it is thus a pleasure to thank him for writing the Introduction. We are indebted to The Football Association for permission to reproduce the relevant pages from their first minute book, and for giving their seal of approval to this publication; at The FA, Ed Coan, David Barber, and Estrella Amigo were especially helpful. Finally, we happily acknowledge our gratitude to Owen Dobbs of Blackwell's, who suggested a book of the first rules of football to us, and who tirelessly worked towards its appearance. This book is dedicated to Cyril McKenzie and to referees around the world.

Foreword

Today we take the rules of football for granted, but I think they are just as significant now as they were in 1863. For me, as well as giving the game its roots, the thirteen original rules embody the spirit or essence of the game. Characteristics such as honesty, courage and skill seem to be taken as a given when I re-read the rules.

When I was playing, the emphasis was very much on abiding by the rules. Players readily accepted the laws of the game and simply played to the whistle. It is fair to say we were not always saints, yet playing by the rules – playing fairly – often set a player or team apart. It was something by which the fans judged us.

In recent times, the game has moved on rapidly, generally for the better. More games are televised, more money is spent, more games are played, even more laws are introduced. In fact so much change has occurred that sometimes I think we are getting away from what the thirteen original laws assume, that to play football all you need is honesty, courage and skill.

This publication reminds us that the original thirteen rules of Association Football are the building blocks of the game. I am proud that England devised these laws and that as a result football has spread around the world as it has. We should not be shy of this achievement but celebrate our involvement and all that it means. We should also recognize that the rules do not simply make it possible to play football; they embody the spirit and heritage of our game.

Sir Bobby Charlton

—KEEPING WARM—

Introduction

I was born in 1939 and I would bet that the first game I played was football. In the kitchen. With a cardboard box, an empty tin and an uncontrollable rubber ball. When I went to the local primary school, playtimes were times for football and after school was more time for football, sometimes deep into the twilight when the ball was a blur and the jackets for goalposts were soaked with evening dew. Cricket took its proper place in the short Northern summer and there was a time for chestnuts, a time for hoops, a time for marbles and a time for bicycles, but football was all the time. A ball, a bunch of boys, flat ground, two equal sides, game on.

When my father came back from the war he took me to see the local professional team, Carlisle United. I was already a follower of my small-town team, the Wigton Wanderers, who copied the Arsenal strip of the 1930s. Clearly that was a divine omen. Through the power of magic and geography, when my son turned eight and wanted to support a team, our nearest, and therefore our natural local team, was and is Arsenal. The last eighteen years as a season ticket-holder have been and continue to be a carnival of earthly delight.

Football is not only a game of skill but also a game of chance, a game of elegance and also a game of strength, a game of long waiting and a game of rapid action. Drama on a field of green. And the game, played world-wide, came into existence only because of a small book, written in 1863. Without that book of football laws, the game would never have been invented and the world would be a much poorer place.

The game of football has, over the last century, totally changed the worlds of sport, the media and leisure. It was able to do that solely because of a book of laws – more commonly called rules – written by a group of former public school men in 1863 in London. Without that book 'the beautiful game', as the great Brazilian footballer Pélé called it, would not have kicked off. Because of that book and the proselytizing enthusiasm of British sailors and merchants and adventurers on their expeditions around the planet, it is now estimated that this year – 2006 – eight out of ten people *in the world* are expected to watch something of the World Cup being held in Germany.

Football is played worldwide by more than one and a half million teams and three hundred thousand clubs. This does not include the hundreds and thousands of schools and youth clubs. There are over five million officials involved in the game. More than twenty million women play the game and their numbers are growing.

It has become part of the national consciousness of almost every country in the world. It would be fair to say that it has become more than just a game: it attracts tribal followings, it produces icons, it provokes passions sometimes not too far removed from extreme politics and devotion which has religious connotations. It is a colossal money-spinner and money-eater on an ever increasing scale. It drives television channels and radio stations and newspapers national, local and specialized. It is a form of universal language, perhaps the most effective form. It has caused at least one war and many battles, often tragic, off the pitch. It has always triggered outbursts of local and national joy, pride, unity. It is colour blind and its influence on breaking down racial prejudice has been strong and widely noted. And all this flowed from the meeting of a few Victorian Oxbridge graduates in a pub in Lincoln's Inn Fields in London in 1863. Before the afternoon was out they had called themselves 'The Football Association' and the Book of Rules was on its way.

This short book made it possible for everyone everywhere to play the same game.

Before 1863, football had been a riot or a confusion.

There are several versions of how the game began. One is that it has its origin in the Roman city of Chester where, half a millennium after the Romans departed from Britain, the Anglo-Saxons played a sort of football with the heads of the conquered Danes. But Professor James Walvin, author of *The People's Game*, has little truck with any of this. 'Games of football', he writes, 'were ubiquitous, spontaneous and traditional … The killing of animals provided people with bladders, unsuitable for most other purposes but ideal to inflate and play with.'

Football emerges more substantially in the written records in the Middle Ages. Professor Walvin writes, 'the game was simply an ill-defined contest between indeterminate crowds of youths, often played in riotous fashion, often in tightly restricted city streets, provoking uproar and damage to property and attracting to the fray anyone with an inclination to violence.'

Help and eventually salvation came from the English public schools. What happened at these schools was that the game took on not one but several shapes. In Charterhouse School, for instance, which was then housed in an old Carthusian monastery in London – a very confined space – the art or craft of 'dribbling' the ball was developed. On the vast playing fields of Eton, the ball could be kicked high and long and it was. At Rugby between the 1820s and the 1840s, the boys caught and ran with the ball and began to develop what would become a separate game but was then called, as they all were, football.

There's a passage in the *Labour Force Survey Quarterly Review* of 1863 which reads: 'the fascination of this gentle pastime is its mimic war, and it is waged with the individual prowess of the Homeric conflicts … The play is played out by boys with that dogged determination to win, that endurance of pain, that bravery of combative spirit, by which the adult is trained to face the cannon-ball with equal alacrity.'

The problems arose when the boys from different schools went to Oxford and Cambridge, wanted to continue to play football and found that because different schools followed different rules, all hell broke loose. This is from the description of a match played in Cambridge in 1848: 'The result was dire confusion, as every man played the rules he had been accustomed to at his public school. I remember how the Eton man howled at the Rugby man for handling the ball.'

There was no difference at that stage between what we now call football and rugby. It became common practice to play half a match by one side's rules, the second half by the other's. That's how half-time evolved.

All these were superseded by a new set of rules on 26 October 1863 in a pub, The Freemasons' Tavern, in Lincoln's Inn Fields, London. There will be those who say that the finalizing of the rules of the most influential game in the world in a pub is deeply satisfying; others might say, 'Typical'. In Britain, at any rate, discussions and disputes on the rules of football have been a feature of our pubs ever since.

On that Monday, representatives, public school men still, from a dozen London and suburban clubs met to sort it out once and for all. This was a book written by a committee – men from a team later to become the Wanderers (a mix of Oxford and Cambridge men), N.N. Kilburn ('N.N.' standing for No Names), Barnes, War Office, Crusaders, Furnival House Blackheath, Kingston School, Surbiton, Blackheath School and Charterhouse School. By the end of the afternoon it was announced that 'the clubs represented at this meeting now form themselves into an association to be called The Football Association'. The process was

launched but it took another half dozen meetings to classify and codify what became the Rule Book.

The central problem was whether a player could pick up the ball and run with it. Blackheath insisted on two clauses: that 'a player may be entitled to run with the ball towards his adversaries' goal if he makes a fair catch' and, second, that 'if any player still run with the ball towards his adversaries' goal, any player on the opposite side shall be at liberty to charge, hold, trip or hack him, or wrest the ball from him'.

At what proved to be the final meeting on 8 December, the Blackheath motion was defeated by thirteen votes to four. Blackheath withdrew from the Association. The laws of the game, which were foreshadowed in the Cambridge Rules, were formally accepted and Association Football was born.

Originally, there were thirteen rules. A few more were added as experience demanded, but those thirteen were all that was necessary to set alight what became the world's favourite game.

The original list is printed on pp. 33–59.

Rule Thirteen can be read as a throwback to earlier, rougher times.

A few more rules were soon added: in 1865 it was agreed that tape should be stretched across the goal posts at a height of eight feet; in 1866 the offside rule was introduced; goal kicks were introduced in 1869; the game was limited to ninety minutes in 1877; and a year later referees were allowed to use whistles. But the basis was well and truly laid in 1863. In 1865, for instance, Buenos Aires F.C. was formed by British residents.

The first game to be played by the Association Rules – the word 'soccer' was already in use, derived from 'Association' – was between Barnes and Richmond. *The Field* reported: 'Very little difficulty was experienced on either side in playing the new rules, and the game was characterized by great good temper, the rules being so simple and easy of observance that it was difficult for disputes to arise.'

The score was 0–0.

In the mid-nineteenth century, textile workers in the north were given Saturday afternoon off. By the 1860s, several other trades had followed. And some, as in Sheffield, gave Wednesday as the half day. It helped the big industries because they could overhaul their machines with a skeleton workforce on that half-day. Clerks and shop assistants had to wait longer for this privilege. There was now time for the game.

Now football began what became a pandemic. Factory teams sprang up in Britain as did pub teams, police teams, church teams, town teams, schoolboy teams, village teams. Spectators began to organize themselves around their local teams. Out of the old playing fields with carts and wagons drawn around them to provide better views for the better off, came new stadiums with cheap tickets. Much of the money was put

back into the clubs by the early gentleman-
ly owners still motivated by philanthropy.
Early commercial developments included
turnstiles, numbered tickets, telegraphic
terminals for posting results to pubs, and
changing rooms. There were rewards, money prizes and payments to players who were
losing paid work by turning out for a local
team. Travel had to be paid for. The day of
the professional came upon football.

For almost thirty years after the Rule
Book was written, the gentlemen amateurs
to whom it owed so much continued to domi-
nate the game. The FA Cup was usually won
by the Old Etonians or by the Wanderers.
Spectators would as often as not turn up to
watch the renowned expertise of a particu-
lar player as to support a team. The game
itself was the thing, the taking part, the
honest effort, the demonstrable skills.

If we are looking for a critical turning
point, 1891 is a good candidate. In that year,
the professional Blackburn Rovers defeated

—WELL DONE MAC!!—

the Old Etonians in the FA Cup. By 1914 teams such as the Eton-educated Corinthians were the last remaining exception in a game which they had passed on to the now dominating working class professionals.

And also by 1914 football was being used for recruitment by the government whose predecessors had condemned it as weakening the readiness for war. In pre-conscription days, the government decided to use the football ground as a recruiting ground. An agreement between The FA and the War Office stated 'Where football matches are played, arrangements are to be made for well-known public figures to address the players and spectators, urging men who are physically fit, and otherwise able, to enlist at once.' Posters went up. One, rather carelessly phrased, reads 'Do you want to be a Chelsea Diehard? If so, join the 17th Battalion Middlesex Regiment ("the Old Diehards") and follow the lead given by your favourite football players.'

By November 1914, according to *The Times*, more than 100,000 men had volunteered through football organizations. Two thousand out of the 5,000 professional footballers had joined up. And football was played up to the front lines – employed as a cheap and effective way to keep the men fit.

There are several stories of football in the First World War. They appear as tiny dabs of light in the Stygian slaughterhouse of trench warfare. A Captain Nevill used to lead his men over the top with the rather obvious but suitably sporting signal of kicking a football towards the German trenches. There's a painting by John Singer Sargent, *Gassed*, which shows a number of injured soldiers approaching a dressing station. Behind them other soldiers play football: the contrast and the connection could not be clearer.

Most famous, however, are the 'Christmas Truces' between the German and the British soldiers. Some are apocryphal, others undoubtedly happened.

Kurt Zehmisch of the 134th Saxons records in his diary: 'The English brought a soccer ball from the trenches and pretty soon a lively game ensued. How marvellously wonderful yet how strange it was. The English officers felt the same way about it.' It is doubtful whether the English had more than a few words of German, even though a Germanic dialect was and remains the backbone of the English language. But football, to use an appropriate even though hackneyed word, transcends language.

In 1888 the Football League was formed with twelve teams: Aston Villa, Derby County, Notts County, Stoke, West Bromwich Albion, Wolverhampton Wanderers, Accrington, Blackburn Rovers, Bolton Wanderers, Burnley, Everton and Preston North End – all from the North or the Midlands.

In 1889 a league, the oldest association outside Britain, was formed in Denmark. Three years later, Argentina was the first country outside Britain to have a national championship. A year later, the movement hit Italy, with Genoa the first club. And just before the end of the century, in 1898 the number of official laws reached the grand total of seventeen – still the modern number.

So it went on, so it goes on. In 1920 the first football pools coupon was introduced, in 1927 the first league match was broadcast on radio, in 1930 there was the first World Cup (Uruguay 4, Argentina 2).

Football drove out other games, which was often a cause for anxiety and even mourning. In Tsarist Russia, for example, where the game was introduced by Lancastrian mill engineers, the game was by the 1890s already attracting crowds of 30,000, and it all but eliminated traditional peasant sports. British influence on what became the Russian national game later disturbed the communist authorities and history was rewritten to demonstrate that its growth was inextricably linked to the triumph of the Russian proletariat.

It has been linked to more than that. The war between El Salvador and Honduras in 1969 is known throughout South America as the 'Football War', which led to about six thousand deaths in a series of three World Cup qualifying matches.

There is, however, and I think this a prevailing view, an opinion well if rather euphorically presented by Simon Kuper, writing before the 1994 World Cup in his book *Football Against the Enemy:*

> The World Cup will be what it always is: a carnival of peoples, the one place where Swedes, Russians, and Tunisians will hug and kiss and swap shirts on neutral soil. Even Americans will be allowed to join the party. If US forward Clint Mathis scores a beautiful goal, Iranians, Iraqis and Libyans will rave about it. Soccer has many uses, and one of them, fleeting as it may be, is universal love.

Football has been used and still is used to bring nations together. At its most effective the success of a national team brings a sense of national coherence in nations old – for instance, England when it won the World Cup – and new – Brazil, for example. Much more importantly in Brazil, in Peru and in many other countries, a football team bridges or ignores the race divides. It is colour blind. When, for instance, in the 1970s, the Brazilian military government attempt to 'whiten' the national team, there was a huge popular and successful demand for the return of the black players who had been and were soon again selected on merit.

Extreme reactions can be very funny. Kapuscinski Ryzzard, in his book *The Soccer War,* writes:

> After Mexico beat Belgium one–nil, Aynto Mariaga, the warden of a maximum security prison … became delirious with joy and ran

around firing a pistol in the air and shouting 'Viva Mexico!' He opened all the cells, releasing 142 dangerous hardened criminals ... A court acquitted him ... he had acted in a patriotic fashion.

Football now rakes in billions of pounds. The huge success of Sky Television in Britain was driven by football. Rupert Murdoch saw its power, bought key rights at what seemed exorbitant costs, but football drove what had seemed a sick enterprise to compete with and outgun the leaders of British broadcasting. Other channels vie for football rights. Advertisers assert that only sex beats football in shifting products. American companies – Coca-Cola, Master-Card, McDonald's – bid for space in football games with advertisements never seen back in the USA. Stadiums are built for hundreds and thousands of pounds, players are paid £50,000, even £90,000 a week, ticket costs soar. Tabloid newspapers make their profits through football coverage. Football merchandise is big business even in countries where football is not yet strong on the international scene.

It is there in the surest test of all – the language. A football: in Spanish, *el futbol, o futebol* in Portuguese, *le football* in French, *der Fußball* in German. Goal: *un gol* in Spanish and Portuguese and Italian. The Captain: *el capitan* in Spanish, *o capitão* in Portuguese, *le capitaine* in French, *der Kapitän* in German, *il capitano* in Italian.

As Mark Ives, The Football Association's County Business Development Manager, said after taking a football mission to children in Botswana, 'All you need is a ball and some kids and they all start speaking the international language of football.'

Provided they play by the Rules.

Footballers are now compared to Greek gods. Football stadiums are often called the cathedrals of our day. Football is routinely described as an art, its theatricality, its human triumphs and tragedies thought by some far to surpass the dramatic feasts available on the stage. It can obsess children, as I know, and continue to obsess them when, as apprehensive adults, they turn up to watch their team and are mesmerized by a game of such simplicity and yet such complicated possibilities, of such dynamism confined to such a small space and of such a power to affect thousands and move them to roars of rage, of delight, even of ecstasy, that you can only wonder once again at the irradiating impact of a book, and such a small book, a Book of Rules put together in a pub in London by a dozen English gentleman enthusiasts in 1863.

A HARD STRUGGLE—

The Rules of Association Football 1863

Meeting 1st Decr 1863 at the Freemasons' Tavern

In December 1863 the founding members of
The FA met to finalize the rules of football at
a tavern in Lincoln's Inn Fields in London.
The handwritten text from the notebook held
by The FA, in which they recorded these rules,
and defined both basic terms and the rules of
The Football Association, is reproduced on
the following pages.

1

The maximum length of the ground
shall be 150 yards, the maximum breadth
shall be 100 yards. the length & breadth
shall be marked off with flags, and the
goals shall be defined by two upright
posts, 8 yards apart, without any tape
or bar across them

The maximum length of the ground shall be 200 yards, the maximum breadth shall be 100 yards, the length and breadth shall be marked off with flags; and the goals shall be defined by two upright posts, 8 yards apart, without any tape or bar across them.

2

The winner of the toss shall have the choice of goals. The Game shall be commenced by a place kick from the centre of the ground by the side losing the toss, the other side shall not approach within 10 yards of the ball until it is kicked off.

2

The winner of the toss shall have the choice of goals. The game shall be commenced by a place kick from the centre of the ground by the side losing the toss, the other side shall not approach within 10 yards of the ball until it is kicked off.

3

After a goal is won the losing side
shall kick off and goals shall be chang

After a goal is won the losing side shall kick off and goals shall be changed.

4

A goal shall be won when the ball
passes between the goal posts or over
the space between the goal posts (at
whatever height), not being thrown,
knocked on, or carried.

4

A goal shall be won when the ball passes between the goal posts or over the space between the goal posts (at whatever height), not being thrown, knocked on, or carried.

When the ball is in touch the first
player who touches it shall throw it
from the point on the boundary line it
left the ground, in a direction at
right angles with the boundary line

5

When the ball is in touch the first
player who touches it shall throw it
from the point on the boundary line
where it left the ground, in a direction at right angles with the boundary line.

6

When a player has kicked the ball
any one of the same side who is nearer
to the opponents goal line is out of play
and may not touch the ball himself
nor in any way whatever prevent any
other player from doing so until the ball
has been played: but no player is out of
play when the ball is kicked from behind
the goal line.

6

When a player has kicked the ball any one of the same side who is nearer to the opponent's goal line is out of play and may not touch the ball himself nor in any way whatever prevent any other player from doing so until the ball has been played; but no player is out of play when the ball is kicked from behind the goal line.

In case the ball goes behind the goal
line, if a player on the side to whom the
goal belongs first touches the ball, one of
his side shall be entitled to a free kick
from the goal line at the point opposite
the place where the ball shall be touched—

If a player of the opposite side first
touches the ball, one of his side shall be
entitled to a free kick (but at the goal only)
from a point 15 yards from the goal
line opposite the place where the ball
is touched. The opposing side shall stand
behind their goal line until he has had
his kick—

In case the ball goes behind the goal line, if a player on the side to whom the goal belongs first touches the ball, one of his side shall be entitled to a free kick from the goal line at the point opposite the place where the ball shall be touched. If a player of the opposite side first touches the ball, one of his side shall be entitled to a free kick (but at the goal only) from a point 15 yards from the goal line opposite the place where the ball is touched. The opposing side shall stand behind their goal line until he has had his kick.

8

If a player makes a fair catch he
shall be entitled to a free kick,
provided he claims it by making a
mark with his heel at once; and in
order to take such kick he may go so
far back as he pleases, and no player
on the opposite side shall advance
beyond his mark until it has kicked.

If a player makes a fair catch he shall be entitled to a free kick, provided he claims it by making a mark with his heel at once; and in order to take such kick he may go as far back as he pleases, and no player on the opposite side shall advance beyond his mark until he has kicked.

9

No player shall carry the Ball.

No player shall carry the ball.

10

Neither tripping nor hacking shall be allowed and no player shall use his hands to hold or push his adversary.

10

Neither tripping nor hacking shall be allowed and no player shall use his hands to hold or push his adversary.

11

A player shall not run to advance # throw
the ball or pass it to another.

A player shall not throw the ball or pass it to another.

12

No player shall take the ball from
the ground with his hands while it is
in play under any pretence whatever.

No player shall take the ball from the ground with his hands while it is in play under any pretence whatever.

13

No player shall wear projecting nails, iron plates, or gutta percha on the soles or heels of his boots -

13

No player shall wear projecting
nails, iron plates, or gutta percha
on the soles or heels of his boots.

Definition of Terms

A Place Kick

is a kick at the ball while it is on the ground, in any position in which the kicker may choose to place it.

A Free Kick

is the privilege of kicking at the ball, without obstruction in such manner as the kicker may think fit.

A Fair Catch

is when the ball is caught, after it has touched the person of an adversary or has been kicked or knocked on by an adversary, and before it has touched the ground or one of the side catching it; but if the ball is kicked from behind the goal line, a fair catch cannot be made.

Hacking

is kicking an adversary intentionally.

Tripping

is throwing an adversary by the use of the leg.

Knocking on

is when a player strikes or propels the ball with his hands or arms.

Holding

includes the obstruction of a player by the hand or any part of the arm below the elbow.

Touch

is that part of the field on either side of the ground, which is beyond the line of flags.

Rules of
The Football Association

1. That the Association be called "The Football Association".
2. That all Clubs of one years standing, be eligible for Membership.
3. That the Subscription for each Club be £1.1s. per annum, payable in advance.
4. That the officers be a President, a Treasurer, and a Secretary, with a Committee comprising the beforementioned officers and four other Members. Five to form a quorum.
5. That the Officers be elected at the Annual Meeting by a majority of the representatives of Clubs present, the retiring Officers to be eligible for re-election.
6. That the Annual Meeting be held in the last week of September in each year, at such place and time as shall be appointed by the Committee.

7. That each Club be entitled to send two representatives to all Meetings of the Association.

8. That in the event of any alteration being deemed necessary in the rules or the laws established by the Association, notice shall be sent in writing to the Secretary of the proposed alteration on or before the 1st of September in each year; and the terms of the propsed alteration shall be advertised in such sporting newspapers as the Committee may direct, at least fourteen days prior to the Annual Meeting.

9. That each Club shall forward to the Secretary a statement of its distinguishing colours or costume.

By order.

Freemasons' Tavern,
Great Queen-street, London.